To Be a Kid

Maya Ajmera and John D. Ivanko

with a foreword by Chris Kratt and Martin Kratt of the PBS shows *Kratts' Creatures* and *Zoboomafoo*

SHAKTI for Children

Charlesbridge

W9-BWJ-508

To be a kid in . . .

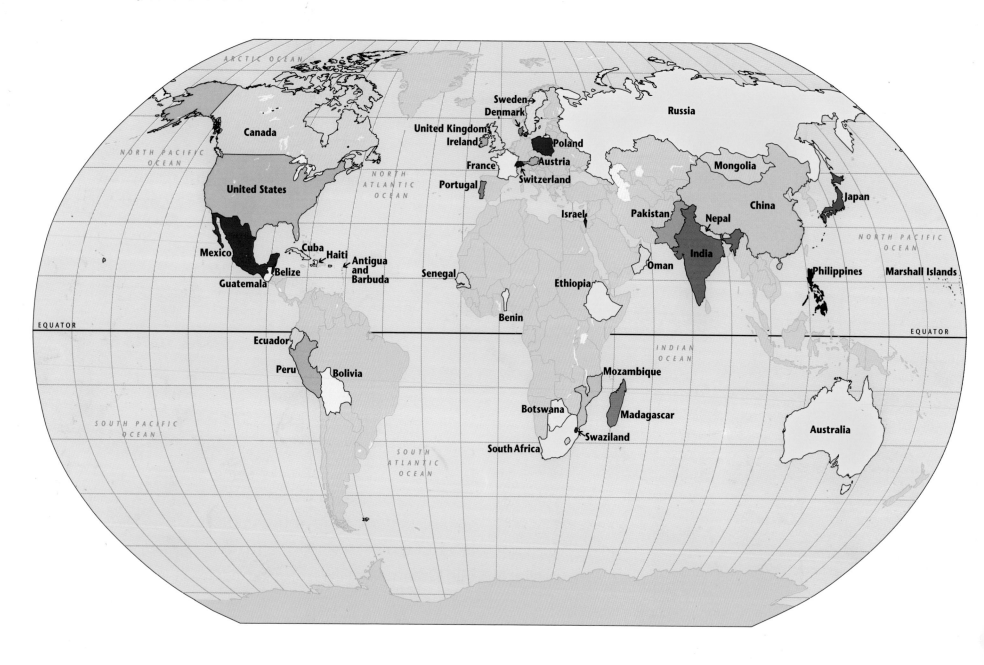

Nepal

Philippines

Israel

To be a kid means going to school

South Africa

Pakistan

Russia

and learning lots of new things.

Philippines

Ethiopia

Marshall Islands

To be a kid means walking home together,

Bolivia

South Africa

sharing a story,

Guatemala

Ecuador

having a cool snack on a hot summer day,

Denmark

Bolivia

or marching in a parade.

United States

Ecuador

Botswana

To be a kid means

India

Cuba

playing ball,

Mexico

Antigua and Barbuda

running races,

Mexico

France

going skating,

Switzerland

Sweden

riding a merry-go-round,

Austria

or playing a board game.

Nepal

France

United States

To be a kid means painting beautiful pictures,

South Africa

Poland

India

sharing the joy of music,

Peru

China

or dancing your

Philippines

Ireland

heart out.

India

United States

United Kingdom

To be a kid means taking care of animals.

United States

Japan

India

Haiti

Mongolia

Ecuador

To be a kid means goofing off

Madagascar

South Africa

and acting silly.

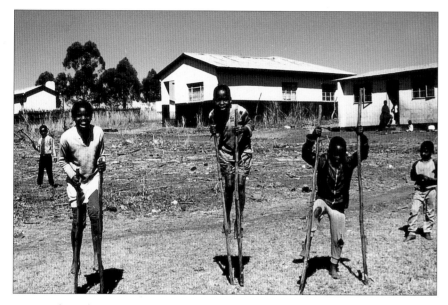

Swaziland

Guatemala

Belize

To be a kid means making friends

China

Benin

Australia

that last forever and ever.

Oman

Mozambique

United States

Being a Kid

Families Even though families speak different languages and express things in different ways, love and care and kindness are shared across cultures. You may have one parent or two. You may live with grandparents or your uncle or your cousins. But no matter what, families are there to help you grow and to protect you from trouble.

School Your never-ending questions can be answered at school. Some classrooms have long desks and chairs, others have computers and chalkboards. Some can be outside, and some are even at home. Wherever you are, your teachers help you learn about the world and encourage you to discover and explore.

After-School Activities With friends from your school or your neighborhood or your village, adventure is just around the corner. You can read your favorite book or march in a parade or take music lessons. You might like volunteering with your scout troop or just exploring the world around you.

Play Through sports and play, you learn new talents and skills. Around the world, boys and girls play sports like soccer and cricket and baseball. They run really fast in races and balance themselves on skates. Playing helps you learn how to cooperate on a team and to be your best.

The Arts Have you ever danced an Irish jig or listened to music from a different country? Imagination and creativity take many forms. From painting to music to dancing to writing, in every part of the world there are special ways to express your creativity.

Animals Many of you have animals that you take care of. Whether you have dogs or cats, horses or monkeys, you feed them and give them baths and care for them if they are sick. You also play with them for hours and hours. Having an animal is a lot of responsibility, but it can also be a lot of fun.

Fun Around the world, everybody likes to have fun. You might enjoy climbing a tree or swinging on a jungle gym or just making funny faces. Goofing off at the beach or balancing on the seesaw with your friends makes you smile and laugh until your stomach hurts.

Friends Friends talk and laugh and work and play wherever they live. They share discoveries and secrets and favorite snacks. They help each other by understanding and listening to each other's problems. Friends are a very important part of life.

To Be a Kid is dedicated to the "seventh generation of children on earth."

Acknowledgments

I wish to thank friends and colleagues at SHAKTI for Children. Special thanks to John Ivanko for bringing this superb project to my attention; all the photographers for their belief in this project; Olateju Omolodun of SHAKTI for Children for her creative input; and the Board of Directors of SHAKTI for Children. I would also like to thank Brent Farmer, publisher of Charlesbridge, who recognized the power of our vision and welcomed us to the Charlesbridge family.—*Maya Ajmera*

I wish to thank my wife, Lisa Kivirist, and my mother, Susan K. Ivanko, and all the children of the world who opened their hearts and welcomed me with smiles and led me into their joyous world of youth. And most importantly, it is such a refreshing pleasure and creative inspiration to have had the opportunity to work with Maya Ajmera, to share in her vision for what the world can become, one child at a time.—*John Ivanko*

We would both like to thank our wonderful editor, Kelly Swanson, and Mary Ann Sabia, vice president of Charlesbridge, for their wisdom and direction on *To Be a Kid*. For their help and words of wisdom, thanks to Peter Blomquist, Christina Prather, and Howard Schultz of Starbucks Coffee Company; Susan McLennan, Chris Kratt, and Martin Kratt of Paragon; and Elaine Griffin.

Financial support to develop this book came from the Teddie and Tony Brown Fund, the *echoing green* Foundation, the Grace Jones Richardson Trust, and the Z. Smith Reynolds Foundation.

We are grateful to the many people who contributed to this book. Any errors that remain in the book are the responsibility of the authors.

Photographs (counterclockwise by spread): *Front Cover:* © 1998, Jon Warren; *Back Cover:* © International Public Affairs Branch of the Australian DFAT; *Title Page:* © Elaine Little; *Foreword:* all photographs © Paragon Entertainment; *Family:* © Steven G. Herbert; © John D. Ivanko; © Elaine Little; © John D. Ivanko; © Mary Altier; © Elaine Little; © Elaine Little; © Stephen Chicoine; © John D. Ivanko; *School:* © Elaine Little; © Siteman/Monkmeyer; © 1998, Jon Warren; © Isaiah Mosteller; © Elaine Little; © Mary Altier; *After School:* © John D. Ivanko; © Elaine Little; © John D. Ivanko; © John D. Ivanko; © John D. Ivanko; © John D. Ivanko; © John D. Ivanko; © Jane Lombardo; © John D. Ivanko; *Play:* © John D. Ivanko; © Mary Altier; © Jesse Ward Putnam; © Steve Macauley; © Steve Macauley; © Maya Ajmera; © Elaine Little; © Elaine Little; © John D. Ivanko; © Maya Ajmera; © John Moses; © John D. Ivanko; *The Arts:* © Elaine Little; © Elaine Little; © Michelle Burgess; © John D. Ivanko; © John D. Ivanko; © Elaine Little; © Watson/Childreach; © MacPherson/Monkmeyer; © Mary Altier; *Animals:* © John D. Ivanko; © Maya Ajmera; © John D. Ivanko; © Lisa Ponzetti; © Richard A. Foster; © Elaine Little; *Fun:* © Gretchen Young; © Elaine Little; © Watson/Childreach; © John D. Ivanko; © Christopher C. Szell; *Friends:* © Stephen Chicoine; © International Public Affairs Branch of the Australian DFAT; © 1998, Jon Warren; © Elaine Little; © Christine Drake; © Robert Hitzig; *Copyright Page:* © Lisa Ponzetti.

SHAKTI for Children is a nonprofit organization committed to teaching children to value diversity and to grow into productive, caring citizens of the world.

Copyright © 1999 by SHAKTI for Children
Foreword copyright © 1999 by Chris Kratt and Martin Kratt
All rights reserved, including the right of reproduction in whole or in part in any form.

Developed by SHAKTI for Children
Box 99350, Duke Station, Durham, NC 27708
(919) 956-9606
www.shakti.org

Published by Charlesbridge Publishing
85 Main Street, Watertown, MA 02472
(617) 926-0329
www.charlesbridge.com

LIBRARY OF CONGRESS CATALOGING-IN-PUBLICATION DATA
Ajmera, Maya.
  To be a kid/Maya K. Ajmera, John D. Ivanko; foreword by Chris Kratt and Martin Kratt.
    p.   cm.
  Summary: Text and photographs from countries around the world illustrate some of the activities children everywhere have in common.
  ISBN 0-88106-841-1
  1. Children—Social conditions—Juvenile literature.
  2. Children—Social life and customs—Juvenile literature.
  3. Children—Pictorial works—Juvenile literature. [1. Manners and customs. 2. Cross-cultural studies.] I. Ivanko, John D. (John Duane), 1966–. II. Title.
  HQ781.A27   1999
  305.23—dc21   98-17930

Printed in South Korea
10 9 8 7 6 5 4 3 2 1

To Be a Kid was designed and composed in Bitstream's Calligraphic 810 by Kachergis Book Design, Pittsboro, North Carolina.

This book was separated, printed, and bound by Sung In Printing, Inc., South Korea.

Other SHAKTI for Children Books

Children from Australia to Zimbabwe: A Photographic Journey around the World by Maya Ajmera and Anna Rhesa Versola (Charlesbridge, 1997)
Xanadu, The Imaginary Place: A Showcase of Writings and Artwork by North Carolina's Children edited by Maya Ajmera and Olateju Omolodun